# *illusion and reality*

*by*

*David Edward Hope*

©*David Edward Hope*

*ISBN 0 9504749 1 6*
*First Edition*
*1998*

*Published by Prior Park College*
*Bath. BA2 5AH*

*Printed in Great Britain by*
*Butler & Tanner Ltd., Frome and London*

*A collection of fiction and poetry,
dreams, ghosts and wake-up calls.*

*Proceeds donated to the
Prior Park College Tanzania Project.*

*For all my loves*

salt

# SALT

She carried all her ghosts with her, when in to the hills each day she walked, and on to the cliffs she climbed. I could not find them though for when she looked my way, her smile would pierce my soul and I, blinded, my heart impaled on the steel of her eyes, would try to endure within her flame. It is the sea that she always wanted, that is her country. She was an ocean woman and loved to sit in those outrageous heights of the coast where her tears could water the ground and in the springtime flowers would grow from the fissures beneath her feet. When dolphins leapt past at Sennen she would rush to the water's edge calling, a heartrending edge to her voice as, dreaming, they passed her by.

They leave behind her forlorn figure as she wearily shifts back to the vertical plane, as though someone she loves has just gone by without acknowledgement and the remainder of the day becomes brooding and dark inside her. She is a creature of the sea, rather than the crag, and would spend her time under it. The summer she spends beneath the waves, dancing in the tides and beckoning me in. I hate the feel of sand between my toes and walk the beach in trainers and socks, foolishly stepping back from the waves as they dart at me, the sound of her silver laughter sensual in the breaking waves of passion that come later, lying in the gentle loving mockery of my fears. "I will teach you to love the sea", she whispers and curls herself tight into me. She is my friend and my love but I still cannot banish the past that hangs around her and keeps me apprehensive in her company.

We met in that most ordinary of places, the indoor climbing wall, and shared a rope or two as she began to climb. I had some knowledge, and not a little experience, and would check her knots and point out the holds and occasionally tighten the rope on some hanging struggle for her. The shadows in her eyes held me in thrall but the past she kept closed so I could not find the way to her. That winter I spent my days on crags and moors and coasts, keeping company with her distant being, close but never near. Bit by bit a trust began to show with jigsaw pieces added, tiny fragments slipping out of climbs done before, and of partners who, well, seemed to not be there any more. She had climbed certainly, but that I ignored in my teaching for it brought me close.

A while ago, I had a photograph before my mind, now newly remembered. It was of a beautiful woman framed against a cliff, her loved ones about her. Her eyes were open but in them her spirit lay closed off to all outside. She sees not the family around her and I find that my finger cannot pin the image down. It is in my memory from some time ago and haunts me daily, the eyes probing into my present, following wherever I sit. I am conscious always of their direction.

The North Coast is a forbidding shore in the winter yet I visit it often, spinning down my rope into the depths of the cliffs to run before the snatching waves and find climbs to fill my soul. Gowla is magical when the seas run wild and I often sit and watching the spray fly 300 feet above the summit towers. A quiet pint is routinely sampled in the local and there, chillingly, I sense the frame upon the wall, and within it, against a lifeboat, sits my love. In chill anticipation the tale unfolds of a lost husband claimed in storm, a son who followed, and a father washed to shore a bleeding hulk many Octobers before.

I cannot see the reefs of pain causing the wreck of her soul for the photographer has scavenged her beauty from the waves' scattered offerings. And thus I dwell on the coast for a while, searching deeper beyond the barrier's mystery. Accounts of many storms and whiplash winds and tales of ropes hanging off cliffs, of brave men with women waiting for ever, watching the sea for remnants of former lives to surface so their peaceful rest can be claimed. The tale unfolds a hundred years or more before and my torch of discovery lights a mystery, a mystery of a lady who left to go up country so the local records say, "Bristol way", to find and live in the blessing of a spinster aunt, a mystery of a beautiful, sad lady with chestnut hair and steel splintered eyes and a smile of such huge generosity that I cannot but help fall in love again and again, tying my knots within the embrace of her intense presence.

"I may drive down to Devon and sit by the sea", she writes. I offer to come but, No, she is adamant. It is October and there are relatives to visit whom I may not yet meet. "One day," she promises, "I have told them I have met a delicious man and they wait upon me as I tease them a little more. It is my way".

She did not come back.

Months passed, and then a year, and the Autumn is here again. Exploration calls and I am by myself this weekend, my friends gone north for a taste of gritstone's bite at their knuckles, leaving me lonely in my searching.

My pint sits untouched now and I stare morosely at the frame on the wall. The pub is cool, a new landlord unaware of its history but glancing askance at me as my eyes remain glued to the eyes behind the glass. The photograph is faded now, the eyes opening in on closed walls yet in their place lie fallen stones from whence my dreams tell me the cascade of my words broke through a year before. My imagination blurs the vision and I fancy I see an eyelid tremor and feel a sense of hiding there as the firelight behind reflects on my spectacles.

In the morning the beer lies stale upon my tongue as I prepare for the abseil, prospecting a likely looking corner, glimpsed briefly from a precarious grass lip a hundred yards away. A check of the knots and the belays and then I was ready.

I eased back into the strain of the rope and satisfied that all was complete, stepped out, not looking up. For a few brief moments all was well, then..... I was flying backwards, the sea two hundred feet below. I automatically twisted in the air, looking for the ledge I knew lay below in an almost unconcerned effort to spot the grass for digging my hands into, knowing that I could arrest my unscheduled descent if I hit it just right. A crunching jolt brought me upright, scraping shoulder and skull against the rock. The belay caught my attention, only five feet above. Was that all it was? I gave a nervous half laugh-come-cough and saw that only one half of the double fisherman's knot was tied. Luckily, the knot was on the far side of the karabiner and that had jammed so catching and holding me. Shaking, I placed my forehead against the cool of the rock and sighed with relief.

She came to me then, flooding back into me and I started, feeling the grass brush against my cheek but so much softer this was and scented as her hair. The chuckle in her voice snatched at my heart and there, there above me she sat, the white Victorian high collar, laced and pure above the grey worsted dress in the photograph. Smiling down from the ledge, leaning towards me, her hand on the rope she reached out with her fingertips. A trickle of saline fear slid down my cheeks as her tears fell upon my tongue. The blood from my grazed cheek lies burning on my lips. "I need yours too", she whispered, the salt of her sorrow biting sweetly as she spread her crying across my face.

"Beloved", she murmured, and taking my hand in hers pulled me to the knot. I watched smiling as my fingers slowly, inevitably, unfurled the rope and, gazing beyond myself, watched the end slipping softly through the silver link. I do not know how far I fell but some time later the sea took me, and below, resting in her liquid arms, I found my beginning.

*songs from a gentle man*

*XXIII*

*If*
*tomorrow*
*you said*
*stop*
*I would smile for you*
*tenderly kiss you*
*cradle you for one last time*
*and turning away*
*would travel the heavens*
*searching*
*for my childhood's end*
*searching*
*for the million fragments*
*of my broken heart*
*each one*
*weeping*
*your name*

*Firstlove*

*What force is this
that memory thus draws forth?*

*I see a purse
centred on a table,
pairing hands, fingers turning,
enfolding, teasing, tingling,
at each tip that touches
talking opposites
each side turning, tumbling
the purse over,
each hand trembling
as closer contact
skin brushing
voice deepening
eyes matching
light glimpsing
proposed tendernesses
shared in gentle laughter
as the purse lifted
then fell
to find the fingers
scrabbling for control
as minds provoked
and hearts dance.*

*Fingertips join,
briefly
then again
and again
they do not want to leave
the blood singing
the soul flying
on the chuckles of her breath*

*so soft, so sweet.*

*I see her smile even now
thirty years on.*

*I see her rippling waters flow
and hear the shining of her care.*

*Even now I sense her hand in mine.*

*Though held I back
from saying
love you,
love me.*

*Hands (one)*

*You say you have farmer's wife hands.*
*Images of crudeness conjure peasant roughness,*
*harsh labour,*
*torn nails with omnipresent dirt*
*bemoaning such strength inherent.*
*And yet how wrong, how demeaning.*
*Your hands are forged through love,*
*child protectors,*
*slender like hardy willow*
*yet strong of skill,*
*positive of touch.*
*Earth hands,*
*goddess hands of care.*
*I sense that touch now in my memory,*
*cool, firm, shocking cold,*
*a chill of crystal, heart-embedded,*
*threaded carefully, my eyes' needle*
*searching, craving that touch in my solitude*
*while around us people chatter*
*in a crowded office.*

*Those hands could do a lot of damage,*
*or cradle a host of unfulfilled loves*
*in careless pursuit of a listener.*

*Would I were that farmer.*

*Hands (two)*

*The cold stops the rose's breath:*
*sharp gasps,*
*crystal fear on the air.*
*When fear is the mind killer,*
*strangling hope at source,*
*recite my given litany*
*"he loves me, he loves me, he loves me!"*
*Feel the dread recede*
*and with the awful thoughts soon gone*
*the bloom returns in peace,*
*the pain dulls,*
*the empty hollow that is grief*
*sifts slowly away from the heartsease*
*of my haven's shore.*

*Your thorns can not shred my gentling hands*
*for I will sap their fright*
*and soften soon the brittle shell of that stark form*
*to tempt the new dawn out*
*and share my spring of love.*
*Each gash your thorns provoke*
*sends out my soothing balm*
*to quench the thirst of torn emotion.*
*You are so vulnerable.*
*(Behind me a fear lurks.*
*Will I soon be the cause of your pain,*
*in the intimate dance of our circle game?)*

*Touching*

*a touch defined*
*is*

*(i)*
*to put one's hand so as to meet, thus*

*why then, when met*
*does our flesh*
*flare blindingly through*
*all intervention*
*shock senses to ecstasy*
*sear our bones and weld our forms inviolate as one*
*for that brief second alive*
*in conjoined souls?*

*is*

*(ii)*
*to strike lightly, affect with such stroke*

*why then, staggering, do I faint,*
*as knee meets back*
*in companies various*
*torn by lack of sight in you*
*framed in doorways distant.*
*Stroking shoulders freely accessed*
*wildly affected, stunned in euphoric agony*
*thriled to existance' core.*
*How such a bland phrase?*

*is*

*(iii)*
*to affect with tender or painful feelings*

*why then, what can I add to your touchstone's*
*test*
*marking our alloy with*
*scars of uncertainty*

*is*

*(iv)*
*to be slightly crazy*

*why then, in my incessant search*
*for you*
*does my madness seem the only sanity here*
*as I stand feet away*
*the air crackling*
*years apart*
*the rulebook cackling.*
*You are but one small step away from my collapse*
*into your shelter.*
*This small dark room is so comfortable.*
*Must I come out?*

*First Song*

*the desert woman dreams of rivers
flowing homeward to her sea
bathing in his eyes' salt waters
cleansing woes his soul to free*

*in this great tide of love requited
gives she him all truth and trust
he would pledge for love united
every oath and promise just*

*he can dream her through his hours
she can hold him for a while
she most beautiful of flowers
folds her petals around his smile*

*sadness lies about them always
as they search for time to be
with each other for their life days
she in him and him in she*

*Sonnet Three*

*How did I journey on my way to you,*
*Led on by glance and smile and gentle touch,*
*To find one eve a frightened soul in view,*
*And discover a kindred spirit such;*
*While in myself to justify my care,*
*I dream of days to meet just free from fear,*
*Wherin my heart's desire I can share,*
*And hope to live and thy great gift revere?*
*You did for my life better days provide,*
*In clement passion and in warm embrace,*
*A sheltered arbour within which to hide,*
*And feel your fingers ease my tired face.*
    *So peaceful in your cradle do I lie,*
    *I gladly would remain here till I die.*

*Daughter - Blessing*

*In a sea of glass
a child spirit leaps
and trails behind
her crystal laughter
dancing through my tears*

*From a sky of fire
a phoenix flame aspires
and wings towards
her golden promise
healing all my fears*

*LIII*

*Be not afraid of the world,*
*be it so full of noise and harms,*
*that jump and start to cause upset*
*and undermine your days of peace.*
*When voices shriek as cats*
*and gossips cry their insidious wares*
*think not of envy's sullen hordes*
*that lack all generous thoughts*
*nor dwell on meanness sour that feeds*
*on jealousy's reproach.*

*Think then of those that give you love,*
*that live within your spirit's bounds,*
*who share your sun and moon and stars*
*and comprehend the splendour of your smile.*
*Their day begins and ends in truth*
*that radiates full fervour in your eyes.*

*Each word you speak, each glance, each thought*
*are instruments you play with sure touch.*
*My strings hum gently as music you perform*
*my every care intrinsic in your harmony*
*Your heart's pure clouds upon me drop*
*such gentle rain*
*each fragile touch a gift of sleep*
*to live in waking dreams of you.*
*Each time I wake my thoughts are yours*
*and when, in waking, sense such loss*
*I so do wish for sleep to dream again.*

## LVI

*In me an animal crouches,*
*alert to the sound of a civilisation*
*that touches only to corrupt.*
*I listen for the rustle of a branch, the breaking of a twig*
*to signal the hunter's threat.*
*In the sky, a distant scream of a gull echoes*
*against the background rumble of the thunder reckoning*
*or is it the waves crashing through the wrecking of my mind?*
*My Indian sign is Coyote,*
*the joker.*
*I know how to hide behind the darkest bush*
*and watch the exquisite birds appear*
*on the water, one by one.*
*Breaking free from cover I leap in jest;*
*all the bright birds but one*
*flee from the river*
*leaving only the grace of the stillwhite swan.*
*Her sky is wide, her blue is depthless.*
*With my eyes trained on her horizons I wait*
*for the dawn to break.*
*I travel through her stillness*
*and enter a silence.*
*My dreams tremble like reeds when the winter's wind comes,*
*but soft,*
*her springtime voices call their warmth again*
*to banish my winter ravens.*

*Are there clocks out there to measure our time*
*other than the beating rhythm of two singing hearts?*

*LXXVII*

*landscapes may be:*
*a frame of mind,*
*an arrangement of parts,*
*some movement,*
*simplicity also,*
*right time, right place,*
*to catch the extraordinary moment,*
*light playing fitfully,*
*colour finding density in bleak formatted souls.*

*the final shape appears*
*dark*
*and in its dusk lies intimacies untold*
*in many shades of grey*

*a figure moves softly through it*
*a redgold spark*
*casting light o'er all it brushes*
*to sound out lives in textured days*
*so richly spreading from this angel's feet*
*so strongly watered from her tears*
*that ever seek the seagull's cry*
*until she anchors on my shores*
*where, daring to crush the coal-black sands of misery*
*between strong hands*
*she brings forth shining diamonds*
*and from her fingers' ends,*
*doth blind my eyes in brilliant love,*
*and says*
*"see, your heart, 'tis mine"*

*LXXVIII*

*a tigress prowls*
*a foreign shore*
*far from her forest so fond*
*her eyes gaze far beyond the waves*
*into far dawns beyond*
*so then she flies a fixed wing bird*
*to flee the westward sun*
*and seeks the land of concrete and clay*
*the land whence her journey is done*
*whereon with steps of light and quick*
*and breath of haste and greeting*
*she stalks to the lair*
*of her tiger who waits*
*for the fiercelove of their meeting*

*Peace*

*in the quiet of our hearts*
*there is no loneliness*
*just a journey together*
*in the comfort of us*
*we need not talk to feel each other's heat*
*we need not noise to pin our contact down*
*we take an enchanted ride*
*souls enwrapped,*
*fused but free*
*hearts bound,*
*in friendship rare*
*in love, found*
*in our silence, content*

***Thanksgiving***

*Mouse;*
*when I saw you*
*first,*
*timid, drawn and distant far*
*though sitting only within a single span*
*from me,*
*your pain reared in your eyes*
*as you hid*
*behind your meal.*

*Pale? No! the grey of grief, shadowed still*
*lay in your fearing soul*
*and upon your tightened cheek*
*but soon*
*with hesitant if haunted speech*
*you took the days on*
*one by one,*
*your seconds pulsing ever quick*
*with colour skinwards seeping back*
*and when the June sun entered in,*
*full trapped*
*about your flamesheathed crown.*

*Then raindrops danced aloud in song*
*and there!*
*another spring came late*
*but come it did,*
*your blossom smile*
*sought in the light of candles*
*to find a friend*
*and hold a dream renewed*
*of living strong again.*

*Then was your mantle thus enriched
and gloss upon your cheek once more,
a radiance again inside your eye
to shine for me in greeting warm
and in the exploration of
our selves in quiet talk,
I saw another summer burst and life start forth
into the deadness of the tomb
that I once called my heart.*

*Songs from the Desert*

*(i)*

*At eventide the sands whisper.*
*Water is near, they say,*
*each grain conferring, conserving,*
*great forces shaping the dunes*
*while life evolves*
*and under the sun survives.*


*(ii)*

*I see the moon at dawn, hanging close,*
*its coldness, ice cool on the horizon,*
*bringing pale shadows among the erg*
*wherein the living creatures hide*
*before the searing sun*
*brings its shriving heat to bear.*


*(iii)*

*Sinuosity is the desert form,*
*smooth curves touched with delicate fronds of wind born crystals,*
*eddying down the leeward side of barchan or slender seif*
*My desert woman's shape beckons,*
*each bronzed curve,*
*each gliding arc,*
*each golden form of essence earth,*
*the desert landscape,*
*harsh but true,*
*lies waiting my lady,*
*waiting for you.*

*(iv)*

*And so inside the cold night air
my lady walks, her vision fair,
her heart it seeks the living fire
within the depths of her desire,
she sings out loud for her soul to be free,
she sings from the rune-scripted sand of the sea
and in her mind she knows that her home
lies lost in the ripples through which she'll now roam.*

*(v)*

*The camels' shadows trail in caravans
moving steadily onwards to fulfil traders' plans
and the winds' spiral playthings cover their track
so that once they have passed she never looks back.*

*(vi)*

*So to the next morn,
my lady seeks forth
for the new life within her:
she looks to the dawn star rising,
hard red on the crest
of prevailing winds sweeping,
her mind now at rest,
her heart peaceful sleeping.*

*(vii)*

*From dangers of predators
and the air's bitter chill
the night has hid her well.
From the safety of slumber
she wakes and she watches
the world in childlike spell.*


*(viii)*

*The deserts change quickly,
they cannot be tamed,
my lady loves wildness
in her eyes it lies framed.*


*(ix)*

*The sky pushes men hard,
creatures that crawl, search the shadows hungrily
while aloes push their disorderly branches
into the starkest of air.
Even the elephants know with their trunks
the presence of water,
the dryness that blunts.*


*(x)*

*The blacks and the reds that the shadows enhance
lead the wind and the sand in moonlit night's dance,
the air is electric and blue and intense
My lady lives free now, released from pretence.*

*Christmas '96 :symbol*

*look carefully at my face's grain
the lines etched deep
through wind and dust of weary days
and seasons sun-baked rains,
and therein see my depth
my form and fire,
my creation,
embered far beyond the shining surface
of my new sought self.*

*its touch is soft.
smooth your fingers o'er its patterned shadows
and let your lips taste sweet,
upon the walnut knots
that draw your fingers in
to contour across my profiled curves*

*breathe deep my spinal musk
and sense within
the body of love
you balance upon your palms*

*this, my gift
in love
for you*

*Maidens*

*last year I fell off the end of the world*
*when surrounded by her standing stones,*
*a ring of weathered maidens,*
*she buckled my knees into the easter grasses*
*of false resurrection,*
*her supple body my crutch*
*her smile my spine*
*to keep me upright in my joy*

*the moon hid behind the earth's shade:*
*spurned my light*
*plundered my warmth*
*and left me*
*cold*

*[your quiet song, your guiding light,*
*your urgent touch, your heat in the night*
*all but a distant memory,*
*mind asleep in waking dreams*
*from which*
*I start, and catch a hint, the loss of ancient loves,*
*that not quite remembered song yet still*
*its lovely whispers haunt,*
*its melodies my heart fulfil]*

*the steps to the Minnack lie coldsunburnt,*
*wind teased hair sprays across my face*
*as seagulls mocked*
*and Kynance's quiet cradle protects us*
*forever*

*[the triumphal note of your carpark voice
hand in hand,
"this is us,
us
together,
going out"]*

*and thus enriched
she bursts, split into a thousand suns
never to be joined in truth
or know the picture inside her jewelled frame*

*[the obvious single voice
many faceted,
sings in your sparkling eyes
for me
and in my memories
a million blessings
rain down upon my being]*

*this, with all its faults, is mine
win or lose
my name is Mine*

*Mirror, Mirror*

*mirror lady, mirror lady*
*take my hand and jump with me*
*take my hand, jump through the deep glass*
*seek your soul, your life to be*
*take the risk and jump for freedom*
*take my hand and jump with me*

*fly away so far away*
*from the prison of your past*
*fear's slavery calls no more*
*the pain you flee it can not last*
*so risk the jump,*
*the jump with me*
*fall through my eyes*
*until you're free*

*There find my land of risk and love*
*and call me far from in your heart*
*thus shed the guilt that binds your life*
*see in my glass your chains do part*
*find my broken fragments shining*
*piece them back into my soul*
*call me back from deep inside you*
*find in me your one love whole*

letters from cornwall

LETTERS FROM CORNWALL

Let me tell you about Cornwall. It has been such a slow and long Spring that everything is late. The cliff tops are awash with colour as a result. On the Lizard there is a carpet of Sea Pink and Dog Rose and Eyebright and bigger white flowers that I don't know and rampant something or other fig (bright yellow flowers, and thick succulent leaves and a real threat to the indigenous species - the flower looks a bit like the prickly pear), and saxifrage and bluebells. You should see the bluebells, they're incredibly profuse, blazing in every verge and hedgerow and covering the edges above the ocean. I can't remember when I've seen so many except in my childhood days when my Mum and Dad used to take me to Bluebell Wood for picnics. We always knew when summer had arrived because we'd be off to Bluebell Woods with a party of neighbours, or alternatively, off to Yarm to picnic on the sides of the Tees in the quiet of that traditional, river-encircled, market town with its back wynds and cobbled High Street and stone built bridges and towpath that they used for pulling the ships along when it was a port, many generations of bluebells ago. At Bosigran however, the gorse scorched through the gloom and the mist and the driving rain. That yellow is such an alive colour and the air seemed self-indulgently scented with the honey/almondy fragrance it generates so strongly. Even the lichens seemed to glow with new growth, shining in the wet as the showers blasted us, leaving sparklers glittering in the grass as soon as the sun broke through for a few moments.

The wind was ever present - this is Cornwall! However, it's never out of place; the coast and the cliffs are its homes and it paints so many pictures with every gust and crashing wave that its brutality can always be forgiven because of the beauty it leaves in our memories. As we walked out of the lane towards the Hollywood Walls we looked back north towards Kynance. The bay was boiling with spray and great spumes of grey mystery scudded across the wave tops, caressing the cliff grasses with millions of tendrils of soft moisture droplets. Lion Rock and the Horse headland reared out and up against the onslaught of ceaseless waves, wreathed in diamond smiles as the sun glinted off the ivory fringes of the massive breakers surrounding them. It really was breathtaking, just like that view at Hartland as we rounded the bend and saw the bay beyond, those sharp, jagged remnants of the Culm, resisting forever it seems to us but in reality doomed to fall and then be replaced by others as the shore retreats ever before the sea's power.

I saw a million suns dance with a million diamonds on the water's surface. I saw a million sparkling drops of silver as each wave sprayed its whole into a million salty pieces dashed against the rocky strand. The sky was laced with a million milky wisps of the finest icy fibres to filter out the heat, and the wind brushed past my soul a million whispering times to calm me down in my calling out for you. My friend understood and so we sampled climbing games in vertical playgrounds, embroiling minds in thoughts that tied us into life, each second gone, each inch moved up, all motion binding thought to action secure, for one short careless act meant harm beyond recall if we should put a foot wrong or place protection carelessly.

There were two climbers on Sirius on Coastguard Walls, the route that David and I did the last time we were there. It was good to get a different, and very impressive, perspective with the waves leaping around at the base of the climb, the occasional one snatching high towards their feet but never quite having the power to deliver a reprimand for daring to be there that day. As we sat on the belay ledge above Hollywood Walls I got lost in the timeless reverie that always grips me when I watch the sea. I'd watch the slow swelling crest rising out of the occasional rock beyond the shore then sweep forward gathering speed and bulk to just before descent, thumping and rolling and bruising against the platform and pools protecting the cliff. There, it would roar and rush in circular fury, flinging itself back and forth, driving higher to reach us but too far gone in its rage to reach us today. As the backwash fled, so it would meet another rushing in and occasionally the angry collision would blast jets of fuming foam towards us, spattering flecks of weed and salted drops that would wet our lips and shift us back from the edge before we got a soaking. Every now and then a monster would make its presence felt, far, far out, its turbulent passion sensed rather than seen before the roaring sound picked up to a greater crescendo and then we would run to the edge to feel its glory on our faces as it smashed down in ecstasy, spurting its energies towards us as if to say, "Join me, I am beauty, I am strength, come to me and sleep in the comfort of my arms, you will never know love without the power that I can give."

Its siren song is demanding, tempting, deep and oh, so seductive. There is such a sensuality about it that suddenly I am finding my mind hundreds of miles away with you breaking above me in waves of fire and delight and I am shaking and longing to feel your arms about me once more. Like the sea I can wait until the moment of my breaking swell arrives on the sweetness of your shores.

So I drove back alone and then you called and then I called you back and all that was left of the evening was my lonely room.

*songs from a broken heart*

*LVII*

*You want the sea,*
*that is your country.*
*The stingrays guard you well,*
*and protect your fragile form*
*from the harpoon's barb,*
*the predator's jaw.*
*You circle in fun*
*whirling,*
*through dark passages in the coral,*
*the whip-tailed child beside you,*
*leading to spiralling pockets of glorious colour.*

*You are of the greatest deeps;*
*where all your mind's oceans*
*fly from your mouth,*
*as old, old stories*
*from the shivering hulks,*
*holding all the loves you contain,*
*breaking from the chest*
*coming to light,*
*bursting splinters of silver on the surface*
*to fill your creel with fish.*

*The whale translates the ray's song*
*"No matter how hard I try to forget you,*
*you always come in to my mind.*
*When you hear my broken song*
*you will know that I weep for you"*

*In the murmuring of the night,*
*will you listen for my fractured voice*
*to heal with your kiss of peace?*

## CV

*And so
your divine wind has ceased
to blow
to send its heat and fury
far beyond your world
to touch my inner senses true
and bring my life to fruit.*

*The coldness of your centre now
is hard to see
from some months back
but you are ice when ego rules
and stack your frozen ramparts high
each brittle stem
each blackened thorn
now hardened sharp to ward away
my heart's soft love*

*Its blood seeps from its many scars
and lies in congealed hopes
upon the bitter ground.*

*Your door rings shut
upon my ears
and one by one
the lights within your glacier eyes go out*

*I turn and turn but find no way to go
and point my dreams away
towards another lost horizon*

*Mill Farm*

*days of peace*
*harmonic quiet*
*come stealthily upon*
*the soul*
*in despite*

*the tiny laughter of a child*
*the soft drizzle*
*of a lowering cloud*
*brushing sweetly*
*over the brow of a hill*
*cools the eyelids sore*
*and clothes in shining gems*
*the broad leaves of the moorland turf*
*the tinkling bells of erica*
*the seeded browns of bracken carpets*
*and the hunt's call on the distant wind*

*there was a leaf on my window this morning*
*a yellowing sycamore,*
*tossed there by the night wind*
*through it shone the grey sky*
*behind which hid a sun*
*it glowed on through my day*
*a tridented sentinel*
*warding off the fears from the days to come*
*the wind did not think*
*I needed the support so*
*by lunchtime it was gone*
*stripped from my glazed expression*
*as the sleep of tranquillity closed around*
*and did my soul protect at last*
*and did my heart release thus give.*

*Sounds*

*Do you know the cruellest sound?*
*The click of a telephone dying in an ear*
*the silence of jealousy inflicted to wound*
*the rage of a woman in fear profound*

*Do you know the coldest sound?*
*the lack of an answer or comment or thought,*
*emotion intense, the chillness of death*
*so speechless that warmth runs away from her breath*

*Do you know the most lifeless of sounds?*
*the weariest remark, the frown in a throat*
*the listless disinterest, the yawn meant to balk*
*the boredom of apathy, the aversion of talk.*

*Do you know the saddest of sounds?*
*the choke of his answer cut down by her scorn*
*the scream in his stare as he looks in his grief*
*and the love he is speaking cut off by hate's thief*

*Do you know the unhappiest of sounds?*
*the wind round his collar, the moan in the ground,*
*the cold seeping silence, the ice of her tone*
*his "I love you" halved by the click of her phone.*

*Do you know the hollowest of sounds?*
*the end of transmission, the buzzing background*
*the shock in his face as he looks in his hand*
*shaking with tears in the phonebox he stands*

*Do you know the sound of his life?*
*the woman he loves, who said she'd be wife*
*but facts are facts, there is nought there but strife*
*in misbelief with his words she is rife*

*Do you know the sound of his death?*
*it lies in assertions of faithless intent*
*yet he weeps in his mourning for the silence she shows*
*while devouring the love that his heartache still grows*

*Alone, Again, Tonight.*

*The softest pain that sadness is
seeps gently through all times
unexpected it appears
every space wreathed as if by mist
insubstantial
incomplete
losses never to be found but vaguely grasped at,
the wisps
slipping from hands
fingers flailing but ever failing
to hold and thus falling
falling,
falling,
remembered days lie strewn about feet in the fluttering winds
gifts of love
slowly re-appearing for a few moments
tender memories of giving
of commitment promised
eternity
now gone,
now gone,
aimless regrets drift in the fragrance of a remembered night,
moon enhanced light framing
that look of absolute love now denied,
now hidden,
now refuted
in the fallen promises of friendship.*

*There is a lost soul somewhere,
slowly sifting through leaves of many colours,
trying to find
the gold again,
trying to wash the earth clean through,*

*all soil from fingers cleansed,*
*grasping at the weakest straws,*
*promises breaking apart in the deftest of touches,*
*the loudest of calls,*
*the firmest of embraces,*
*splintering puffs of organic motes flaking into the air*
*as the final straw is clutched*
*and disintegrates*

*this life is done.*

*the weakest fabric of flesh disperses*
*to find new growth to nurture*

*there is in life much love to give*
*why then does no-one want*
*in need to find*
*life's truth*
*within we?*

*Did We?*

*we breathe the same air don't we?*

*the tang of salt catches in our throats*
*sweet, rich, pungent with the living seas*
*our lungs burn*
*in the spraydashed waters stinging reproach*
*deep gulps, bottlegreen breaths,*
*flecked with the spittle of a cream breaker*
*rack our straining ribs*
*my heart rocks steadily,*
*shrugging off all hammers*
*turning aside the ocean's blows*
*with superficial ease*
*(while beneath, the waves quarry away,*
*successful erosion hidden)*

*we hear the same song in the night don't we?*

*lightening sears and singes the clouds,*
*crackling loud in the repressed returns of thunder,*
*the shattering air breaking loud about*
*our ears' tender shields*
*each flashing rent within the storm's coarse rage*
*replaced by dawn's soft chorus*
*of trees, whispering our secrets to the world*

*we shine, seeing under the same sun don't we?*

*the rainbows dance upon our stage*
*each day, each day where prismed flames*
*break up into each blazing shred*
*each spectrum thread of radiant light*
*each falling pool of glowing green*
*to frame about the brooding tor*
*a masted, island ship adrift*
*in Somerset's grey shallows*

*we smell the same mother earth don't we?*

*Gaia's full fragrance, clay heavy, dew soft,*
*issues from the fresh ploughed drills*
*brown and bronzed in the slanting spears of sun*
*that pick the dark earth out*
*from the seagulls' dazzling, raucous white*
*life hangs heavy in the expectant air*
*as new lambs take their first tottering steps*
*towards their too brief lives*

*we taste the same bitter-sweet fruit, don't we?*

*moments that melt on the mind*
*taste sweeter still in memory*
*(for that is where they now live,*
*the poison of bitter thoughts*
*neutralised by patient time)*
*enhanced with the spice of secret looks*
*daring touches, and the silence left*
*upon the telephone's tongue*
*an aftertaste reminds us that life remains*
*to be endured without love*

*we tasted the same bitter-sweet fruit, didn't we?*
*lived a life together at least in spirit,*
*didn't we?*

*LXXXIII*

*Did you hold the rainbow in your hand today?*
*I did, I did, but the colours ran between my hard and calloused fingers*
*and of all the silken threads now left*
*only the lifeless linger*

*Did you catch the skylark's song in your ears' pitch today?*
*I did, I did, but the song crashed round the booming drum*
*and of all the gossamer notes now gone*
*all but the dischords ring dumb*

*Did you catch the eyebright's smile within the morning dew?*
*I did, I did, but the gathered drops from my scaled eye fell*
*and of all the sweet iris reflecting the blue*
*only the bloodshot now tell*

*And did you catch the falling firehawk between your outspread arms?*
*I did, I did, but its dive now stiffened in spiral death did lurch from side to side*
*and in the soft thud of its end my heart*
*screamed in its extinguished pride*

*Honey, Candles, Flowers*

*There is a picture
of irises blue,
pale and indigo,
shot through with the bright sun of yellow
glowing on your table.*

*Look closer and you will see
some purest white.
Therein lies your integrity.
It is the core,
your very centre,
the purest colour of life
composed of all the rest.*

*Do not split it by the prism of mine eye.
Let it lie shining,
burning as your candles,
lighting the way
to you.*

*It is blameless as are you.
It burns cleanly as do you.
And sometimes the air
is filled with whispers of tender care
as you speak to my dreaming self.*

*I hear you talking
through their flickering tongues,
telling me slowly of the joys to come,
and in their perfumed garden,
I sense the bees,
gathering honey
for the long winter.*

*Don't Go*

*You
whom tears suit so well
wear
your salt diamonds
without stain*

*They do not fall as seeds
except to grow in my heart
where my tongue has taken them
in lieu of love
where my kisses have followed
your tracks
deep into my soul*

*Behold
your face is cleansed
of memories
I have them safe
within my reservoirs*

*one day
the load too great becomes
and crashing through the sluices
flood
the waters of my life*

*I can not hold the deluge back
as my tears now echo
"Don't go"*

*Too late!
The dam is dry,
the paradise of roses,
shrivelled.*

*C*

*In the desert the slipping of the sand
beneath the straining feet of oryx
heralds the dawn breaking.
A wind comes,
softest breeze flowing to bring in the sun's
trumpeting brass
of light glaring harshly back
at a rejected world.*

*Its soft dune curves are edged with shapes of glass,
each honed to slice a breaking heart
into the many mirrors of your shattering smile.
Above, the hydrogen furnace picks out each weakest life
and snuffs it mercilessly out.
A camel's ribs gape starkly
into the maws of a vicious love.
No silent graveyard this
as shrieking airs
strip past
and vulture like
pares every bone of flesh.*

*In the distance there is the gleam of something white.*

*Look close:
it is my bleached heart,
a trophy
on the wall of your life's oft injured soul.*

*Don't worry.
It will be gone soon.
Your wanton sands will bury quick
the memory of my too tender care
then wait to trap
another weary traveller in your pain.*

*Anniversary (one)*

*did you hear that scream tonight?*
*loud*
*primal*
*it rent the very air*
*in its tortured self*

*did you hear my scream tonight*
*pitiful*
*atavistic*
*it fell upon deaf ears*
*through my soul's despair*

*you didn't even watch me go*

*16.1.97*

*CXXVI*

*(With apologies to Katharina von Schlegel, b. 1697)*

*Be still, my soul: though far from you is she;*
*bear patiently the cross of grief and pain;*
*leave to your God to order and provide;*
*in every change he faithful will remain.*
*Be still, my soul: your best, your special friend*
*by thorn-paved paths will lead to joyful end.*

*Be still, my soul: your Love will undertake*
*to guide the future as it has the past.*
*Your hope, your confidence let nothing shake,*
*and now all mysteries shall be clear at last.*
*Be still, my soul: the tempests still obey*
*her voice, that sang so sweet before their play.*

*Be still my soul: respect once more you earn*
*when broken promises to scissors turn*
*and slice apart the strings of puppet dance*
*manhood regained, life's gift will soon be yours*
*Be still my soul: all hollow phrases matter nought*
*for in your heart lies freedom's timeless port.*

*Be still my soul: the hour is hastening on*
*when we shall be forever within the whole,*
*when disappointment, grief and fear are gone,*
*sadness fled, love's pure joy restored.*
*Be still, my soul: when change and tears are past,*
*all safe and blessed we shall meet at last.*

### CXXIX

*she wants not a love,*
*nor companion*
*nor friend*
*all she demands*
*is a puppet*
*to bend.*

*straw wires*
*broken promises*
*never mend*
*but fine scissors do make*
*for those strings*
*to rend.*

*tangled limbs*
*shattered heap*
*on the ground*
*listen hard*
*broken heart keening*
*is the sound.*

*April*

*in sadness, peace is finally found,*
*the grief not passed but within its place*
*lies acceptance,*
*quietly assimilated through events,*
*unrelated truamas flying free,*
*and, about me are others,*
*people in lives beyond my remit*
*who in their independence*
*prove to me that life is there*
*to live*
*beyond the grave*
*of your loving execution.*

*I shall wear your gifts in grace,*
*and honour the spirit*
*of a life passed in joy,*
*consigned to its proper place.*

*Remembrance - Bleeding Still*

*Poppies dance on our histories,
wind withered petals
announcing their falling,
by soft puffs of dust, exploding
through the soil's summer dryness.
Beyond, the clouds fragmented,
lie loves lost and lives lived,
dreams gone in the raw drizzle
of drifting fears,
sadness lingering until
another golden harvest comes
threaded through with soft bedded rubies,
each one a grave
for your countless loving promises of
always.
Goodbye. My gentle lady's dead; goodbye.
Goodbye my lost love, mourning.*

*My tears disturb the fertile soil once more
and in your holy ground
another seed stirs.*

*soulsong*

*at times my soul appears not
to be
at home
and then the pain
of loss
bites deep*

*explain? I can not tell,
yet know my heart
seeks oft its gaping void
while waves of sadness
o'er me sweeping still
hint soft again the fragrance
of my memoried song
your waking dream forgot*

*10.12.97*

# a sea change

A SEA CHANGE

It had been a good week with our confidence rising continuously as we pushed our grades beyond former limits. The final day was to be fitting then, and, awakening to the same blue skies of previous days we lingered over breakfast and a second mug of tea. Even on such a day, the Great Zawn is a forbidding place but we blended with ease that summer, fingertips and fists hardened to its coarse crystals and searing cracks. We scampered rapidly over the approach, anticipating, driven almost, to the abseil point.

We pulled the ropes through.

There were no hints, no shivers of apprehension, nothing to indicate the day ahead but as we stood on the edge of the crevasse I was vaguely aware that the sea had a rougher edge to it, a few white horses, a choppier, irregular rhythm, not quite in tune with this sun-washed morning. Not threatening but disturbed. Ignoring it we stood on the other side of the crevasse joking about how desperate we'd first thought that jump to be years ago, now just routine. Soon, the gear racked, he went to work from the boulders on to oddly wet rock to reach the foot of the groove. It was, as the guide stated, greasy but also running with water against all expectations. A slipping foot brought a quick runner and a few feet further, another, as the slime oozed an uncomfortable atmosphere into the air. For some unaccountable reason I checked the belays though there was no need. A fleck of spray caught my ear and salt water flicked into my left eye, stinging. The day was hot, the sky cloudless but I felt chilled. The rope slid out a few more feet and grunts and swearing from above gave evidence of an unexpected thrutch on this supposedly straightforward pitch. Although not concentrating fully on the rope I mechanically inched it out. The shine was off the start of what should be a great day. A scatter of spray dotted the back of my T-shirt and its companion swell took my left foot. I swore and shook the saturated leg, taking a step back and glancing seaward. The vagueness of my earlier apprehension distilled into something firmer for the sea was not playing the game today as the weather was. Besides, we'd got the tide right as well so why am I getting wet? The air had changed too, the quality of the sound, deeper, booming, oceanic. And then came the first wave. I recoiled in shock, soaked to the skin, staggering back a little and inadvertently tugging the rope. A strangled cry of surprise came from above, demanding attention and no pulling. I apologised and stepped back onto a higher boulder, freeing more rope, keeping a wary eye to the sea. I added my own comments of haste too, amazed at the sea's mood change, rapidly altering to ones of shock and cursing as another, bigger wave slapped me to the bed of the zawn in an angry swirl.

"Make it snappy. I'm getting soaked down here," I called.

A grunt and a few more feet, and then the belay ledge, but not before two more wrathful swipes had left me shivering, scraped and a little worried. Both of these had hit the groove above me and I had to climb the bloody thing. I ought not to have looked back out to sea but I was under compulsion, sensing fully what was going to be there. A black, brooding sea was rolling great crashing fists of Atlantic into the mouth of the zawn, hiding the lower sky and darkening the already gloomy floor. A lull in the waves allowed me to get in to the groove and up it a few feet. The first runner wouldn't come out and I caught the full force of the wave and a mouthful of salt, swallowed in the gulp of a breath. Coughing and retching I shouted for a tight rope which was duly delivered with much mirth from above. The next one drove the breath from my body and and I noticed with grim satisfaction that the spray had caught him as well. 'Serves him right for laughing,' I chokingly thought, and then realised that the waves should not be reaching him. Forty feet up and that wave reached him? In disbelief I watched myself as if from afar as the water casually brushed my hands and feet from the rock in the next rush. I dangled, twisting in the rope, and now, very much frightened. Fighting for breath, every time I opened my mouth I drew in water and spat and choked and gasped frantically.

"For Chrissake take in the effing rope," I screamed, not realising that he too was dripping. The ledge arrived abruptly, courtesy of the swell, lifting me and throwing me a crumpled scrap at his feet. I grabbed automatically at the belay rope and hauled myself to my feet as he tied me in.

"What the hell's going on?" he shouted, trying to make himself heard above the roar.

"I don't know and I don't care," I yelled back into his ear, "but we're not going to climb out of this at 6a so we'd better figure out how to get off."

It was difficult to communicate because the sea was thumping and clawing at us continuously. I looked up through salt-smeared eyes to see them breaking twenty feet above us. Realisation came quickly. We had to get across the traverse to the crevasse and then reverse the jump to the abseil platform. It was difficult to think straight or to organise, each wave beating us against rock, expelling breath by sheer force, and numbing us with increasing cold. Breathing was an epic in itself as each blow submerged us for what seemed like hours while lungs shrieked for air. With eyes closed under each onslaught it was difficult to gauge the time for the next air so a throatfull of water would leave us rasping in oxygen, unable to time the next hit or gasp, catchhing us in mid-breath and thus exhausting us further. We were just hanging from the belay as it seemed pointless to try and stand on the ledge but we somehow couldn't work out the next stage given the fury of our surroundings. It was then that I began to wonder whether we might not make it out at all.

Time was suspended as we grimly fought to stay upright in each rush of the ocean. Somehow we established the idea that we would have to traverse across the teeth of this foaming monster and found ourselves counting the seconds between each breaker. The first attempt was a skidding lurch across the wall, lunging for any hold to purchase enough time before impact. The next wave took him with one hand clawing vainly at a crack, and bodliy flung him upright some ten feet until the rope stopped his rise. The force on the belay plucked me off my feet and as I lurched sideways the plate locked and he dropped, catching a glancing blow with his thigh before going under the next wash. I hauled him in and held him tight with one arm against the ledge as the next wave hammered over us and seemed to keep us submerged for a lifetime. As it withdrew we sank great coughs of air into our lungs, each seeing real fear mirrored in the other's eyes. He got angry.

"Come on you bastard," he raged back at the waters. "Can't you do better than that? Come on! What about a real wetting then?"

I grabbed him by the hair and shook him out of his hysteria, the pain eventually getting through his skull to the brain. Calmer now, though with flecks of spittle flying, he turned to face the gap again. We tried to establish the best landing point on the platform only to realise that it too was raging white with massive sheets pumping back and forth across it, rumbling up the abseil line. But we'd pulled the ropes through anyway and without that security......? One thing at a time now, we've got to get there first, seemed to be a sensible thought creeping over the terror. And so our efforts resumed, assuming an almost dream-like quality with him setting off aiming for the last far point as the sound receded into the background and all that became important was our two sparks flickering, fighting against extinction.

Almost outside ourselves we watched our torn hands clutch and clutch again while the sea played with us, dancing us around on the foam, batting us back and forth between breaker and granite, submerging us until we thought we'd burst, flinging us brutally against the hardened walls of this liquid prison. Our hopes began to fade as salt tears mingled with salt waves, a final enslavement seeming to beckon us nearer. How long, how long? The aches in my body told me that we were still alive. Time did not matter.

Small details stood out. I watched his camera snap from his harness and into the embrace of the sea. I counted our rope's abrasions, waiting for them to reach the inevitable, almost natural separation and end. My watch, a gift, had disappeared long ago. I sucked my torn knuckles, wondering at the life in their salt taste and once, only once, found my thumb in my mouth as my eyes, storm wide in wonder, watched a wave of hideous cruelty pin him into the crystal map far above me before slowly withdrawing, leaving him to scrape sickeningly down the wall. A peculiar mental calm fell about us now as we held each other for a while. In the next effort he almost made the ledge before the crevasse only for him to slip and fall away. A despairing lunge with his left hand caught an edge though and a great sobbing moan escaped his lips before the next wave caught him and flung him on and beyond the crevasse to flounder among the surf on the platform. I screamed at him.

"Get up, geeet uuuuuuuup! You've made it. Get to the wall before the next one."

He hadn't heard I'm sure but instinct saw him crawling slug- like on hands and knees, only to be bowled over and thudded sickeningly into the back wall, the swash almost pulling him back. "Please noooo," I whimpered to myself, "Please don't take him back. Pleeeease no!" I cried on in silent misery but the waves relented and he appeared, staggering on one knee, his arm over a good lip in a hollow, slowly making ground across the platform.

I don't recall how he made the last few yards to the foot of the exit route but somehow he was tied on with nuts and laboriously pulling in the ropes against the snatching of the waves. I didn't want them to come tight. This place was my harbour, my security. So what if each wave tore my feet away? To commit myself to a swim in these towers of fright seemed an absolute lunacy. I had to talk myself into it. Chech your harness. Check! Are the knots OK? Yes, OK. Which nut will come out easiest, that has to be the last? Ok, it's that one so take the other out now. Come on! Oh, come out you bastard! I collapsed at the futility, weeping in rage, barking laughs and spitting out each wave as it engulfed me. You stupid fool, I thought. Just untie and go, leave the sodding nuts, treat yourself to some new ones.

In the event the sea took my hand and as I unclipped the final belay I was flung into the air and descended head first into its clutches. He told me later that I was screaming in abject fear but I have no recollection. I was just thinking that I hate swimming, that I can swim but I dislike it as an activity and that this was a stupid way to die. I came to, bobbing around, gasping, thrashing the disoriented surface, seeing only white and blue around me. Where was the crag? And then a mule kicked me in the back as I was slammed against the wall below the crevasse. I hung briefly on the now tight rope as he held me and managed to turn and face the ledge, having enough presence of mind to watch the next wave drive in and jump on it, arms flailing wildly. I dropped on to the platform and with a combination of scratching, dragging and crawling, made it to his belay. We were still being hit but now the full force of the attack was being curbed by the wall of the platform. At least we could breathe in relative comfort without fighting to stay on our feet so slowly I aided my way up the exit route, often slumping into the slings to rest. God, how I hurt. At the top it was some while before I could trust myself to stand and fix the belay, coming to from my daydreaming with his calls finally reaching my ears. God, I ached. Spent but secure I brought him up and we slumped on the upper ledges and slowly stirred.

Pushing the tears from my eyes I glanced across at him as he dragged himself into a sitting position and sagged back against a boulder. He tried to grin. I noticed that he'd chipped a tooth and his gums were flecked with red above a swollen and discoloured lip. A sliver of blood and mucus was smeared across a cheek from his nose and a dull wet glow of red in his matted hair was beginning to seep out over his left temple. One sleeve of his T-shirt hung by a couple of threads above a rent seam, almost torn down to his waist, and angry weals displayed the effects of abrasive granite across his ribs. He swallowed awkwardly, trying to speak but only succeeded in croaking until he'd properly cleared his throat.

"My God," he whispered hoarsely, "You don't half look a bloody mess."

*song from a healing love*

*Anniversary (two)*

*For days now conflict dreams
have stripped my nights,
arguments ringing in my ears,
tieing me to a waking stake,
the hours of morning stolen
in thinking
that a better way exists
but how?*

*A vigil drawn with hardened fright
fights hard
when illusions be the only answer given
by the hanging sword of guilt,
my ego's vicious thought.*

*Then comes my dawn
to bring a proving dream
and passes by attack
for love's true sight
and minutes slide on by
while waking thoughts of you bring sense
and truth burns in
upon my day
and glorious light around me
calms each perfect truth as lilies settle softly
in the peace that knowledge
of my purpose
sets me right.*

*The day hardly begun
the sweat upon my heated body
clings, beaded to my sheeted skin
as I review my dreams.*

*I find forgiveness hard
to bring deep from my mind, but
love's creation
now dispels the mists
and turns aside the mask
of this insane and manufactured world,
this illusion's false parade.*

*I see the innocence
the goodness and perfection
that is love,
that is the truth of you.*

*And in his smile for you,
and in your smile for him,
I see my love's song true.*

*16.1.98*